I AM

Reflections from the Father

CINDY STEWART

WITH KAREN-ELISABETH WILLIAMS

"I AM."

Exodus 3:14

I Am – Reflections from the Father

Invitation

Suddenly I hear the Father speak,

"I AM."

For many mornings after, during my prayer time, Father God would share aspects of what we need to know about Him. He shared His heart for us and how to deepen our connection, transforming our relationship with Him.

This book contains those 44 I AM revelations Father God wants us to know.

To know Him with that deep level of understanding, which leads to oneness with God.

My prayer is that as you ponder each one, you will encounter the Father. And as you do, your relationship with the Father will grow deeper, stronger and more real than the world around you.

Cindy Stewart

I have loved you with an everlasting love.

Jeremiah 31:3 (NKJV)

I AM YOUR
Father
WHO *loves*
YOU.

I created you and formed you
when you were in your
mother's womb.
My love is a part of you.
Feel my love.

(Psalm 139)

I AM YOUR
Father
WHO IS
near your heart.

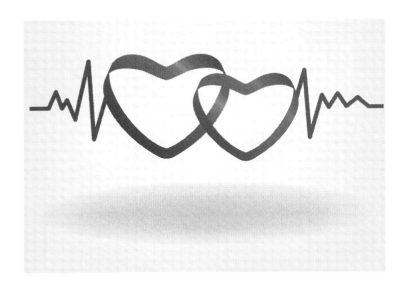

But truly God has listened;
He has attended to
the voice of your prayer.
He does not just listen,
it is that He has taken care of it,
so revere Him, obey Him –
hold fast to the one
who listens and attends
your prayers.

Psalm 66:19 (*ESV*)

I AM YOUR
Father
WHO *hears.*

I HAVE AN ANSWER FOR YOU;
Follow Me.

Therefore, the Lord waits
to be gracious to you,
and therefore, he exalts himself
to show mercy to you.
For the Lord is a God of justice;
blessed are all those
who wait for him.

Isaiah 30:18 (ESV)

I AM YOUR
Father
WHO *waits*
ON YOU.

**I will instruct you
and show you the way to go;
with My eye on you,
I will give you counsel.**

Psalm 32:8 *(HCSB)*

I AM YOUR
Father
WHO *will*
lead YOU.

He gives us the authority to preach
the gospel accompanied with
signs and wonders
in Jesus's Name.

Mark 16:15-18 (Paraphrased)

I AM YOUR
Father OF
authority,
AND I *give* MY
authority TO YOU.

I gave you freedom to choose because I love you.

Galatians 5:13 (Paraphrased)

I AM YOUR *Father* WHO *romances* YOU.

I TREAT YOU WITH LOVE AND AFFECTION.

My love for you is great.
That is what why I chose to
protect you with my Son's life.

John 3:16 (Paraphrased)

I protect YOU WITH *all I am.*

God first spoke to Moses from the bush that burned with fire...

After Jesus ascended to Heaven, God descended upon the disciples in the upper room and the Holy Spirit manifested as tongues like as of fire...

For behold, the LORD will come in fire.

(From the Books of Exodus, Acts and Isaiah)

I AM YOUR *Father of fire.* I WILL BURN YOU UP AND RELEASE *My burning fire* IN YOU. BURN FOR ME.

Burn for Me.

The LORD replied,
"My Presence will go with you,
and I will give you rest."

Exodus 33:14 *(niv)*

I AM YOUR
Father
OF *rest.*

REST IN ME.

God, your God, will restore
everything you lost;
he'll have compassion on you;
he'll come back and pick up
the pieces from all the places
where you were scattered.

Deuteronomy 30:3 (MSG)

I AM YOUR
Father WHO
recovers
WHAT YOU HAVE LOST.

Stop imitating the ideals and opinions of the culture around you... be inwardly transformed by the Holy Spirit through a total reformation of how you think.

Romans 12:2 (TPT)

I AM YOUR
Father WHO
covers YOU.

I WILL TEACH YOU HOW TO LIVE
IN THIS WORLD WITHOUT BEING
FROM THIS WORLD. I AM TRANSFORMING
YOU TO A CLEARER IMAGE OF ME.

Now you have the very light of our
Lord shining through you
because of your union with him.
Your mission is to live as children
flooded with his revelation-light!

Ephesians 5:8 *(TPT)*

I AM YOUR
Father WHO
needs YOU.

I NEED YOU TO ENGAGE WITH ME,
TO FOLLOW ME AND PARTNER WITH ME.
I NEED YOU TO CHANGE THE WORLD
AND IMPACT MY KINGDOM.
I NEED YOU.

As God said: "I will live in them and walk among them. I will be their God, and they will be my people."

(2 Corinthians 6:16)

I AM YOUR
Father
WHO *dwells*
WITH YOU.

**I have given them the glory
that you gave me,
that they may be one
as we are one...**

John 17:22 (*niv*)

I AM YOUR

Father

OF *glory,*

**AND I SHARE MY GLORY WITH YOU.
I WILL MEET YOU WITH MY GLORY.**

For we are God's workmanship,
created in Christ Jesus
to do good works,
which God prepared
in advance for us to do.

Ephesian 2:8-10 (Paraphrased)

I AM YOUR
Father
WHO *partners*
WITH YOU!

His divine power has granted to us all things that pertain to life and godliness, through the knowledge of him who called us to his own glory and excellence,

2 Peter 1:3 (RSV)

I AM YOUR
Glorious Father!

MY GLORY RAINS/REIGNS OVER YOU.
I LOVE YOU.
MY GLORIOUS PRESENCE IS WITH YOU.
I WILL RAIN OVER YOU, ON YOU,
THROUGH YOU.

By Him to reconcile all things to
Himself, by Him, whether things on
earth or things in heaven,
having made peace through the
blood of His cross.

Colossians 1:20 (NKJV)

I AM YOUR
Father
THE *true*
reconciler
OF ALL THINGS.
I AM HERE WITH YOU.

Every good thing bestowed and every perfect gift is from above, coming down from the Father of lights, with whom there is no variation, or shifting shadow.

James 1:17 (nasb)

I AM YOUR

Father WHO

gives life

TO THE BROKEN,

brings healing

TO THOSE IN SICKNESS AND

releases wisdom

IN THE INTIMACY OF ME.

I AM HERE AS YOUR FATHER,

PROVIDING EVERYTHING YOU NEED.

**Though you have not seen him,
you love him; and even though
you do not see him now,
you believe in him
and are filled with an
inexpressible and glorious joy.**

1 Peter 1:8 (NIV)

I AM YOUR
Father
OF *joy!*

I BRING JOY INTO YOUR LIFE,

WITH LAUGHTER, REJOICING,
SINGING AND DANCE.
ENJOY BEING WITH ME; DRINK IN MY JOY!

**The purposes of a person's heart
are deep waters,
but one who has insight
draws them out.**

Proverbs 20:5 *(NIV)*

I AM YOUR
Father
OF *eternity.*

YOU ARE WRITING IN THE ETERNAL SCROLLS FOR
MY PURPOSES TO BE REALIZED.
I AM WITH YOU IN ETERNITY, AND YOU WILL SEE
THE SIGNIFICANCE OF YOUR LIFE
ON EARTH AND WHY I CREATED YOU
FOR SIGNIFICANCE.
EACH DAY WITH EVERYTHING YOU DO,
IT RELEASES A SOUND ON THE EARTH
AND INTO HEAVEN.

David attacked the Philistines
and defeated them.
Then he said, "I watched the LORD
break through my enemies
like a mighty flood."
So he named the place
"The Lord Broke Through."

2 Samuel 5:20 (CEV)

I AM YOUR
Father
WHO *breaks through*
FOR YOU.

Your Father knows what you need before you ask Him.

Matthew 6:8 *(NIV)*

I AM YOUR
Father WHO
answers YOU.

YOU ASK AND I WILL ANSWER.

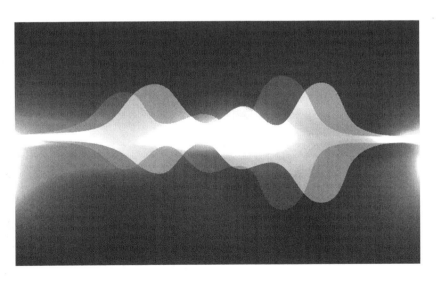

My son, do not forget my teaching,
But let your heart keep my
commandments;
For length of days and years of life
And peace they will add to you.

Proverb 3:1-2 (nasb)

I AM YOUR *Father* WHO *feeds* YOU.

MY WORD NOURISHES YOUR SOUL AND SPIRIT.
I FEED YOU.

**The LORD will fulfill His purpose
for me.**

Psalm 138:8 (HCSB)

I AM YOUR
Father WHO
releases
destiny
IN YOU.

DON'T BE AFRAID
OF YOUR DESTINY.

Yet I know that you are most holy;
it's indisputable.
You are God-Enthroned,
surrounded with songs,
living among the shouts of praise
of your princely people.

Psalm 22:3 (TPT)

I AM YOUR
Father OF
Worship AND
Presence.

I RESPOND TO YOUR WORSHIP WITH MY PRESENCE. YOUR WORSHIP IS AN INVITATION FOR ME TO JOIN.

Set your minds and keep them set on what is above (the higher things).

Colossians 3:2 (AMPC)

I AM YOUR *Father* WHO *molds* YOUR MIND.

MY WORD PREPARES YOU TO LIVE
A LIFE OF DIFFERENCE.
I WILL MOLD YOUR MIND TO BE LIKE MINE.
MY PRESENCE CHANGES THE WAY YOU THINK,
THE WAY YOU LOOK AT THINGS.
YOUR MIND IS LIKE A SPONGE
SOAKING UP MANY THINGS.
IT HAS THE CAPACITY TO ABSORB MUCH,
BUT I HAVE MUCH MORE FOR YOU.
I AM ABOUT TO CHANGE YOUR MIND
TO THINK THE WAY MY MIND THINKS.

And now, O Lord GOD, you are God,
and your words are true,
and you have promised
this good thing to your servant.

2 Samuel 7:28 (NRSV)

I AM YOUR
Father OF
Integrity.

YOU CAN TRUST MY MOTIVES AND MY WORDS.

THEY ARE GOOD TOWARDS YOU AND WILL NOT FALL TO THE GROUND UNDONE. IF I SAY IT, IT WILL HAPPEN. IF I SPEAK IT, IT IS TRUTH. I AM THE FATHER OF INTEGRITY.

All the ways of the Lord are loving
and faithful for those who follow
the ways of his covenant.

Psalm 25:2 (TPT)

I AM YOUR
Father WHO HAS
established MY
covenant WITH YOU.

I WILL BE FAITHFUL TO
WHAT I HAVE PROMISED.

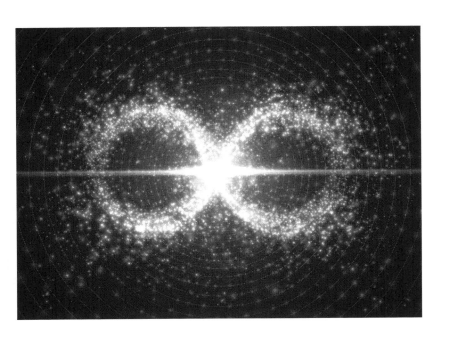

The spirit of wisdom and revelation
in the knowledge of Jesus and
the eyes of understanding will be
enlightened.

(Ephesians 1:17-18)

I AM YOUR
Father WHO
will lead YOU.

FOLLOW MY LEAD.

The Lord your God is with you.
He is a hero who saves you.
He happily rejoices over you,
renews you with his love,
and celebrates over you
with shouts of joy.

Zephaniah 3:17 (GW)

I AM YOUR
Good Father.
I ENJOY YOUR COMPANY AND PRESENCE WITH ME.

My God will supply all your needs according to His riches in glory in Christ Jesus.

Philippians 4:19 (NASB)

I AM YOUR
Father WHO
WILL *provide*
ALL THAT YOU NEED
AND OVER AND ABOVE THAT NEED
— ABUNDANCE.

Both riches and honor come
from You, and You rule over all.
In Your hand is power and might;
and it is in Your hands to make great
and to give strength to everyone.
Now therefore, our God, we thank
You, and praise Your glorious name.

1 Chronicles 29:12-13
(Paraphrased)

I AM YOUR
Father
OF *riches.*

**Now ask and keep on asking
and you will receive,
so that your joy
may be full and complete.**

John 16:24 (AMPC)

I AM YOUR
Father WHO
has it all

AND MY ALL
IS AVAILABLE TO YOU.

---

if GOD is
ALL
you have
Y O U H A V E
ALL
you need

- john 4:8 -

**Now the Lord is the Spirit,
and where the Spirit of the Lord is,
there is freedom.**

2 Corinthinas 3:17 *(nIv)*

I AM THE
Father WHO
HAS *freed*
YOU.

YOU ARE FREE.

**Show Your strength, God,
You who have acted
on our behalf.**

Psalm 68:28 *(HCSB)*

I WILL ACT ON YOUR BEHALF, YOU ARE NOT ALONE.

I AM A
good Father
WHO *will act*
ON YOUR BEHALF.

Now to Him who is able
to carry out His purpose
and do superabundantly more
than all that we dare ask or think
[infinitely beyond our greatest
prayers, hopes, or dreams],
according to His power
that is at work within us.

Ephesians 3:20 (AMPC)

I AM A
good Father
WHO *knows*
YOUR DREAMS AND DESIRES.

The Lord is good.

Nahum 1:7

**You sent Me ... and have loved
them, just as You have loved Me.**

John 17:22 *(amp)*

I AM A
good FATHER.
I AM *your*
GOOD *Father.*

For the LORD will go ahead of you;
yes, the God of Israel will protect
you from behind.

Isaiah 52:12 (NLT)

'For I,' declares the Lord, 'will be a
wall of fire around her [protecting
her from enemies], and I will be the
glory in her midst.'"

Zechariah 2:5 (AMP)

I HAVE THIS.

YOU DO NOT NEED TO WORK,

I HAVE THIS.

I AM THE *God*

WHO *has this.*

I AM THE ONE

WHO HAS YOUR BACK.

I AM THE GOD WHO HAS THIS.

**All the ends of the earth
will remember and turn to
the LORD,
And all the families of the
nations will worship before
You.**

Psalm 22:27 (AMP)

I care.
I care ABOUT
THE NATIONS,
ABOUT THE PEOPLE.

Look down from Your holy dwelling above, from heaven, and bless Your people Israel, and the land which You have given us, as You have sworn to our fathers, a land [of plenty].

Deuteronomy 26:15 (AMP)

I AM YOUR
Father
OF *plenty.*

For with God nothing [is or ever] shall be impossible.

Luke 1:37 *(AMP)*

I AM YOUR
Father OF THE
impossible.

**But God now unveils these profound
realities to us by the Spirit.
Yes, he has revealed to us
his inmost heart and
deepest mysteries through
the Holy Spirit, who constantly
explores all things.**

1 *Corinthians* 2:10 (*TPT*)

I AM YOUR
Father OF
Truth.

**This is love:
He loved us long before we loved
him. It was his love, not ours. He
proved it by sending his Son to be
the pleasing sacrificial offering to
take away our sins.**

1 John 4:10 (TPT)

I AM YOUR
Father
WHO *loves*
YOU.

Bible Versions Used:

Made in the USA
Columbia, SC
08 October 2022